My Pastor's Keeper

Selena Peeks, M.Ed.

outskirts
press

My Pastor's Keeper
All Rights Reserved.
Copyright © 2021 Selena Peeks, M.Ed.
v1.0

This is a work of fiction. Names, characters, businesses, places, events, locales, and incidents are either the products of the author's imagination or used in a fictitious manner. Any resemblance to actual persons, living or dead, or actual events is purely coincidental.

The opinions expressed in this manuscript are solely the opinions of the author and do not represent the opinions or thoughts of the publisher. The author has represented and warranted full ownership and/or legal right to publish all the materials in this book.

This book may not be reproduced, transmitted, or stored in whole or in part by any means, including graphic, electronic, or mechanical without the express written consent of the publisher except in the case of brief quotations embodied in critical articles and reviews.

Outskirts Press, Inc.
http://www.outskirtspress.com

ISBN: 978-1-9772-3317-2

Cover Photo © 2021 www.gettyimages.com.. All rights reserved - used with permission.

Outskirts Press and the "OP" logo are trademarks belonging to Outskirts Press, Inc.

PRINTED IN THE UNITED STATES OF AMERICA

I dedicate this book to the memory of my mother Rosanna Hampton who taught me to never stop dreaming no matter what happens. To my daughter Amber Peeks who constantly reminds me to live life above the clouds. To my sons who make intelligence look cool. To the memory of my grandmother Odie Walker whose strength has taught me to always stand up for myself. Also, to everyone else who has blessed me with your presence over the years. Thank you.

Preface

Father God, in the name of Jesus. Thank you for allowing me to come before your throne of grace. If there be anything in my spirit that blocks this communion with you, I ask that you remove it right now. My gracious, loving father Jehovah, thank you for all your blessings, thank you for sending your son Jesus for the redemptions of our sins, thank you for the use of my limbs, my faculties, my family and the blessings that you have in store. Father, I ask that you use me to carry your message today. That my mind only serves to share your love and grace with this church and give hope and life until your return. In Jesus name. Amen.

As I finish my prayer, I feel someone staring at me. Oh, it's Sister Marjorie, I didn't see her there. After telling me that it's time she turns around and flashes me a slight smile. Then, I notice my wife standing in the doorway with her hand on her hip. I couldn't help but to wonder how long they both had been standing there. Uh oh, what is my wife thinking right now? I hope she's not thinking, of course not. I just shrugged it off because I had to go fulfill my purpose and can't afford to be distracted right now. It's time to do the work of the Lord.

As I walk out to the sanctuary, I hear the thunderous applause. I can't help but to think that this part of the service never gets old.

I love hearing the music playing on Sunday, it's surreal'. So full of energy, so full of the Spirit, so full of life.

My soul has been anchored, my soul has been anchored, Deon the lead singer of the choir wails. Week after week the minister of music always have something to warm the soul. Looking around I am just taking it all in. Sister Longinoe is always beautiful in her interesting yet fabulous hats. The deacons are all casket sharp, all uniformed and in place. The ushers are smiling while greeting our guests and shaking hands. The communion dishes are polished and shining. The sisters did a really great job of cleaning up the throw up from Thursday night. The new organist is amazing, even if he does move his head from side to side like Stevie Wonder. The choir is so strong they are shaking the windows. Tambourines, cymbals, drums, oh my. Umm, the church is full, my heart is full watching all the people coming down to the alter to give their lives to Christ. The Lord is really moving in this place. I got fire shut up in my bones. I can't help to but dance all over this pulpit.

Looking around at the pulpit at the pastors, my fellow foot soldiers, and my wife sitting in the front row look so beautiful. Even the neighborhood children are behaving. I raise both of my hands and start worshipping. Wait, it is all so perfect, almost too perfect. I can't believe this is all happening to me. Sister Marjorie waves at me, in her classic Sister Marjorie's style, and then she flashes another little smile. Just when the praise team introduce me, Sr. Pastor Trevor Sparks, I take a few seconds to take it all in. Then the gunshots rang out…NO!

Scene 1

How It All Got Started

Apostle James is a great pastor, mentor and confidant. I am so motivated to do God's work after watching him speak. Being a Co-pastoring under his tutorage is so rewarding, but I can't wait to become a Senior pastor and one day have my own church. I often wonder if I will be up for the challenge when that day comes. Maybe I should talk to the Apostle about my doubts, pastor always seem to have the answers. After the service, I am in my study contemplating if I am really ready to lead my own congregation. What steps do I need to take? Should I become a sequel to this congregation or start my own? So many questions, so much to consider.

If I am to lead a church, I think I need to take a first lady. The temptations of being in this position and single is bearing down on me like a ton of bricks. 'He who findeth a wife, findeth a good thing, right?' There are plenty of beautiful, God-fearing women in here. How do I choose the right one?

Just as I'm praying for guidance about the many choices Sister Alyssa walks in and interrupt the carnal thoughts that were about to develop (big hips, big lips, big thighs OH MY). I must pray more. Then, I hear the sweetest sound I've heard in months. I swear the Angels were playing harps to the sound of her voice. Hi Pastor, great sermon today, she said. I really liked the part about taking back everything the devil stole from you, she says rather matter of factly. Hey, ever thought about having your own church one day, she asks? Wow, it was like she was reading my mind. As a matter of fact, I have, I answer. We chatted for about an hour which seemed like a lifetime. Small talk at first and then about her life, her dreams, and her goals. The conversation really intrigued me, and I started to bombard her with questions. I admit I wanted to see how she would hold up under pressure.

Were you a good student? How old were you when were you baptized (I was 9 myself)?. Do you drink? Have you ever used drugs? Do you want kids? How many partners have you had? She stopped me right there. She asks what makes you feel that I've had any, she asks with a very demanding tone in her voice and her hand on her hips? Wow can this really be true, I thought. Alyssa is so beautiful. She goes on to explain she's never actually had intercourse. She's 22 years old and a virgin, I think to myself? Now, I am definitely intrigued. Milk chocolate skin, long dark hair, a size 6 and a very nice rack. I am having a hard time focusing on her face as we converse, but I am a gentleman and a man of the cloth. I take a minute to compose my thoughts.

Celibacy can disrupt the brain waves even when you have the best of intentions. Whew, I'm back now. The more we talk I am thinking this girl is amazing. She's smart and beautiful. She knows what she wants. She's ambitious and she likes football. She handled my barrage of questions with poise and confidence considering I was barely giving her a chance to answer. I finally get up the nerve to ask her that one important question. Have you ever thought about being a first lady? Her answer shocked me. As a matter of fact, I have, she answers. Right then I knew it, she's the one.

Alyssa turns around and sees another young lady from our congregation standing in the doorway. Oh, Sister Marjorie. How long have you been standing there? Alyssa asks. Long enough to know you two are planning on having a church one day, answers Marjorie. Marjorie had the biggest grin on her face. We didn't understand what had pleased her so much. Then Marjorie interjects herself into the conversation and start to ramble on and on. OOHH, I'm so excited, she said. I can be your secretary. I *can* be your secretary, right Marjorie asks. I deferred to Alyssa. Well, first lady, I as?. Sure, Alyssa said swiftly. Then we all hugged. Alyssa and I talked every day after that. We wanted to get to know each other on a deeper level. Pretty soon we were inseparable. We were going to the park for walks at least three times a week. We had dinner together every Sunday after church. We went to orphanages together to take the kids on outings and bring them to church. Alyssa even started to travel with me and my brother when she was out of school. Those stolen moments were so special just having her by my side. I have to admit, after each encounter with her I had to take a cold shower and pray about my thoughts. We were spending so much time together outside of the prying eyes of the congregation that we had to be careful not to fall asleep in each other's room when we were travelling. With all this alone time and no one to hold us accountable, we were getting dangerously close to crossing the line. I wanted to experience her body so badly.

Scene 2
Three's a Crowd?

Each subsequent date gets better. Alyssa and I are becoming so close that we can finish each other's sentences. We both agreed that our alone time should be supervised from now on to protect our vow of celibacy and to protect our relationship with Christ. Marjorie and my big brother were more than happy to share the responsibility of chaperoning us at the bequest of Apostle James. Marjorie volunteered to couple-sit first (why am I not surprised).

I love surprising Alyssa almost as much as she likes receiving surprises. So, I called Marjorie to see if she and Alyssa was free Saturday afternoon. Marjorie will have Alyssa to meet her at the church under the guise of going through some financial reports. I will happen to stop by with a stuffed bunny and flowers.

For our newest adventure I reserved a Petal Cart ride at Harvey Orchard that will take on a scenic view of the Orchard that leads to the picnic area for a romantic lunch. Then we will stroll through the orchard to pick our own apples right before we go. I had it all planned out or so I thought. I bought the big wicker picnic basket, matching place settings, tablecloth, and champagne flukes. I packed Waldorf Chicken Salad with croissants, shrimp cocktail, pasta salad, baked Lay's potato chips, strawberries, grapes, of course whipped cream, sparkling grape cider and a bottle of Sweet Red wine. I hurried off to pick up my queen. While on the way to the sanctuary, I realized that I only had two place settings. That's going to make this date awkward with Marjorie sniffing around. Think Trevor, think, I said to myself. Oh, I got it. I placed a call to Marjorie to ask her to gather up a cup, plate and silverware from the kitchen but not to blab it to Alyssa. Marjorie can barely hold water.

The entire drive to the Orchards, I swear Marjorie answered every question Alyssa and I tried to ask each other. Suddenly, I'm not feeling as confident about this date as I was this morning. However, as soon as we parked and entered the Orchards, something changed. Alyssa and I were both engulfed at the sheer majesty of beauty and tranquility that we were experiencing. We marveled at the cod pond, and the butterfly exhibit. We soaked in the laughter of the kids, the birds chirping and the constant joyful chatter. It was like no one existed but us. We had our Petal Bike ride, our romantic lunch and even the apple picking session laughing and just enjoying being together. For some inexplicably reason the sound of Marjorie's voice went unnoticed for hours. It wasn't as intrusive as I thought it might be. Today was a good day.

After our weekly leadership meeting, Apostle James stopped me as I was about to meet Alyssa in the parking lot. Those famous words that still send chills down my spine, 'Son can I have a word?' He must have sensed my hesitancy, because he walked over and grabbed my shoulder and said it won't take long. Apostle James strongly suggested that Marjorie start to accompany me on my conference appearances and speaking engagements that require 'our tender flowers' to be in attendance. Code word for me not being alone with our single parishioners. I guess Apostle James got wind of my relationship with Alyssa before I could talk to him about it. He expressed how disappointed he was that I would withhold that information from him. I had no intention of hiding it, but I just wanted to be sure first. A public relationship could ruin both of us before we know if we really

SELENA PEEKS, M.ED.

want to be together. Plus I didn't need to sabotage my path to becoming a full fledge pastor. I will obey Apostle James's direction to have Marjorie in my hip pocket for the foreseeable future, but that doesn't mean I have to like it.

Scene 3
Unsolicited Attention: I Never Realized I Was So Popular

Immediately after our Orchard date, I gave Marjorie instructions not to mention nor answer any questions about Alyssa and me. Marjorie was given strict directions to forward all questions to me and me alone. I'm guessing that didn't work too well because Sister Longinoe made her way downstairs to my office on her walker to 'have a word' with me. That phrase, along with 'we need to talk', and 'when am I getting some grandbabies' are ones that I am never too excited to hear (especially from mom). Sister Longinoe mentioned the apple orchard and the petal ride. I was dumb founded. I asked Sister Longinoe to give me a few minutes and had Marjorie to get her some water and occupy her for a moment so I could go outside to brace myself for the storm that I knew was brewing.

When I returned about 10 minutes later, I apologized to Sister Longinoe and asked her 'how can I be if service' (A little something I picked up from Apostle James). Under the ever-watchful eye of Marjorie, Sister Longinoe proceeded to tell me about her niece from North Carolina. She is coming in town for a visit this weekend, and Sister Longinoe was hoping that I would be available to show her around. Sister Longinoe went on to explain how her niece Mary, is a very pretty 'Big Boned' girl. She also expressed how smart Mary is and she also cooks. Sister Longinoe then leaned in for the kill by saying, 'you know, Mary is wife material. Those skinny girls can't keep a man strong and healthy'. I didn't know what to say, but I did tell her I would check my schedule and get back to her. As much I hated to involve Marjorie in anything else dealing with my personal life, I had to have her make the call to Sister Longinoe to let her know I would NOT be available.

Over the next few days, I started to receive calls for prayer requests on my personal cell phone. This was unusual because there is a prayer request line that has a prayer warrior available 24 hours a day. I also started to receive home-cooked meals delivered to my office, my house and my mom's home along with a plethora of greeting cards. I could tell that the newfound attention was wearing on Alyssa, who is a very private person. My mom must've noticed because she gave me the 'can I have a word' speech. Mom, ever so graceful asked if she could talk to Alyssa to see how she was feeling about this situation. She wanted to give her a spa day with her friends to help ease some of her frustrations and the tension that has been going on at church. Alyssa and I had started arguing almost daily. At this point I was welcomed to a mud wrestling contest if it got Alyssa away from this drama. I felt like I was living too many episodes of the 'Young and the Restless'.

Scene 4
The Hotel Debacle

I needed to represent Apostle James at a conference in Memphis. The theme of the conference was to showcase the missionary work of young Christians. The title of the conference was 'Junior Warriors Making Moves'. A few others and I had been featured in news articles and magazines for our community involvement about a month before. We all were personally invited to attend the conference to represent our congregation. Every invitee had ten minutes each to speak about how our faith was helping us to make a difference in our community and for humanity. Since Apostle James could not make it, I was given 30 minutes to give a talk on his behalf. The conference was 3 full days with 2 one-hour breakout sessions each day for us to exchange ideas focusing on different areas of ministry (ie. Music, prayer, mentorship, acts of service, etc.).

I called Alyssa immediately upon landing. I promised her that I would call her as soon as I checked into my room. Upon reaching the hotel, we realized that it had been a mix-up in the reservations for the conference. There had been one room booked per church. While the hotel staff and Marjorie were busy trying to secure us accommodations, I made a call to Apostle James to alert him of the situation. During that call we found out that the surrounding hotels were all booked for the same conference. Imagine my surprise when Apostle suggested that we all stay in the room together. I know Apostle James sent Marjorie to make sure that we stayed away from temptation, but I was not at all comfortable with the dynamics of two women and two men sleeping in the same hotel room. What about me, 3 nights with motor-mouth Marjorie? This has got to be a test. One test that I don't care to repeat so I immediately take charge of the situation. First order of business is that we get out of the lobby and up to the room STAT. When we get to the room, I have everyone to get something to drink, breathe deeply for 2 minutes and reconvene in the common area in 10 minutes. I then took a quick glance at our accommodations and noticed that it may not be as intrusive as we all thought. It was a suite with double beds and a sofa bed in the common area of the room that also included a breakfast table with four chairs. The best part was the partition that separated the seating area from the sleeping area.

Once we were all seated (and quiet), I reminded the group that we had a job to do and that everything would be fine if we continued to trust in the Lord. I suggested that we offer a prayer of thanksgiving for our safe arrival and secretly asked for guidance for myself. Just like that, the plan for our stay begin to take shape effortlessly. Marjorie and Denise will have the beds. Marjorie was able to secure a roll-away sleeper from the front desk (for our inconvenience, wink). Daryl and I will take turns on the sofa bed and rollaway sleeper. The conference starts at 9:00am which means we all must be dressed and in the lobby by 8:30 each morning for the driver. I gave everyone strict instructions and even had Marjorie to type up a schedule to put on the wall. This is already an emotionally charged situation. Having expectations in writing ensures there are no discrepancies in time expectations when it comes to the shared areas. The ladies will have the bathroom exclusively from 6:00am until 7:20am. Daryl and I will have the bathroom exclusively from 7:25am until 8:30am. There is a restroom next to the conference center on the next floor in the event of nature's emergencies. Before, I could finish my sentence, I had to ask Marjorie to indulge me for a few minutes before she barraged me with questions. Whew, Apostle James has tremendous patience to deal her so closely. Lord God give me strength. I gathered myself to not show the irritation in my voice and continued with the daily plan. The common area that doubled as the sleeping area for Daryl and I will be available until 11:00pm. I felt that was being generous with us having to share personal space for so long.

After all the commotion, I realized that I had not called Alyssa back after leaving the airport. Shoot, I will call her on the way to the meet and greet. Hopefully, she is busy with Mom again. We have 15 minutes to meet our driver in the lobby. We managed to pull it together and make it to the lobby right before a very impressive limo arrived to pick us up. Two gentlemen stepped out, one holding the sign of our church and the other opening the door. I was flabbergasted. I'd only seen this in the movies and now it was happening to me. It only took about 10 minutes for us to get to the convention center. In all my amazement, I forgot to Alyssa again and I noticed a few missed calls from her. With the events of the previous weeks, I know Alyssa is not happy with me right now. I'll call her as soon as we leave, I know she will understand by me being on my first solo mission without Apostle James.

There was a popular televangelist seated close to our table. He and his wife happened to overhear our (Marjorie) conversation regarding our hotel mishap and how disappointed and disrespected she felt. There was no calming her down even with threat of us both having to answer to The Apostle tonight. The Bishop came over and in a few words was able to calm her, and he invited us back to his home afterwards. Of course, I accepted. The last thing I wanted to report was that I couldn't control the helper that was sent to help us. It felt like having the neighbor's kid throwing food at your white walls. Any action I do can be perceived wrong in an instant. I was so relieved to have a Senior Pastor handling Marjorie that I accidentally fell asleep in his study.

When I woke up it was after midnight. I started to panic once I realized that I slept through my check in call with The Apostle and I had neglected to call Alyssa back. I pleased to know that there was a car waiting to take us back to our hotel. I hurried to call Apostle James for our check-in. I was not happy to find out that Marjorie had been on the check-in call and gave an awful account of today's activities. It took me an hour to assure him that Marjorie's perception was wildly exaggerated, and everything is under control. Although I missed Alyssa terribly, I was not looking forward to making this phone call especially this time of night. I was so thankful that she picked up, but I immediately noticed the attitude in her voice. I was able to keep the questions to a minimum because it was so late. I promised her that I would phone first thing in the morning.

Working on four and half hours of sleep was challenging but having the rules for our cohabitating made the morning less stressful. As I promised, I called Alyssa on the way down to the lobby. I can tell she was still a little upset with me, but she did her best to remain supportive by praying with me. These moments make me love her even more.

The next few days of the conference was remarkably calm and rather enjoyable. We all represented our congregation and ourselves well. I learned a lot of tools that will help me on my journey to become a senior pastor and ultimately leading my own congregation. After all the twist and turns from this assignment, I couldn't wait to get back to Atlanta and hug Alyssa. An 'I'm sorrow' gift was on the agenda for my sweetie.

Scene 5
The Boiling Point

I had Marjorie to call the florist that we normally use which happens to also be a parishioner. Sister Dell always does wonderful work and I know she will create something wonderful to make my honey bunny smile on such a late notice. Sister Dell agreed to get there a little early in order to leave the gift unnoticed. I'm so blessed to have such dedicated sisters around me.

We landed with just enough time to make it to service on time. I checked my voice messages on the way to the church so I wouldn't have any surprises. I knew that Apostle James would be anxious to know how my first assignment without him went so I immediately made a B-line to the Apostle's study to give him the watered-down version of our trip before service. When I emerged from the study to see Denise and two other sisters standing outside of the door, looking like the cat that ate the canary. It looked suspicious but I had to get to the sanctuary to oversee service. I noticed that Alyssa was not in her usual seat. That made me a bit nervous, she did not tell me she was not attending service this morning.

Morning service seemed like it went on forever, and everyone wanted to stop me to ask about our trip afterwards. I took a deep breath and repeated the same account at least 30 times. That took almost an hour and I was hoping Alyssa would still be somewhere in the building. I called, but she did not answer the phone. My heart was racing, and I was sweating profusely. I had to rush to my office to regroup. Hopefully, no one noticed my nervousness.

Once I made it back to my office, I slammed the door and leaned against it to took in a deep breath. While my eyes were still closed, I took a very deep breath trying to slow down my thoughts and my heartbeat. Just then, Marjorie came running down the hall to my study screaming my name. Knowing, I wouldn't get a word in to find out what the emergency was, I clapped my hands three times. (I was trying to incorporate some of the techniques that the televangelist had given me to deal with difficult parishioners). It worked. Marjorie blurted out, 'it's Alyssa come quick'! Now we are both running down the hall toward the yelling.

As I reach the dining hall the scene looked like a schoolyard brawl. My first instinct was to go break it up, but when I got there and saw who was involved, I just froze. Marjorie saw Apostle James first and started to give her side (even though she wasn't directly involved). The ladies were in such a contentious battle that they didn't realize Apostle James was standing there watching the foolishness. The Apostle was standing there with a stern look on his face asking me what happened and why didn't I call him. With all the commotion the thought of alerting The Apostle to the disturbance had escaped me. I had no idea how this all transpired so despite my apprehension, I had to defer to Marjorie.

Apparently, Denise and a few other young ladies from the choir made it a point to discuss the hotel mix-up during our trip. It got so messy that Denise's cousin had convince her to confront Alyssa after service while she was setting up snacks for the junior choirs meeting. Denise stressed the fact they we had been in a hotel room together in Memphis and questioned what type of relationship Alyssa and I had. Marjorie summoned Sister Longinoe, who is a trusted and well-respected member of our congregation, but instead of controlling the situation she added her two and half cents of fuel. Sister Longinoe told the women that I was seeing her granddaughter and the granddaughter agreed. Where is my mother? If there is anyone that can control these women, it's her.

It took Apostle James a few minutes to calm all five of them down even having to threaten reprimands if they weren't quiet. Starting with Sister Longinoe there were five totally accounts of what happened. According to Sister Longinoe, Marjorie alerted her to t he disagreement between Denise, her cousin Deborah and Alyssa in the church kitchen. Sister Longine said she 'had to pray before giving these young ladies guidance'. She went on to say that she heard Denise describe an inappropriate encounter between she and I in Memphis. All eyes immediately turned to me like darts piercing my skin. Sister Longinoe completed her statement by saying she had to explain to all three ladies that I was seeing her granddaughter so none it could be true. Thank God for Marjorie, she quickly disputed that account when The Apostle asked her.

All the other women gave some off-kilter account of a 'relationship with me' and what really happened before the argument. By the time it was Alyssa's turn, I could see the hurt and disappointment in her eyes. Everyone thought Alyssa was about to snap, but she took a deep breath and stated matter-of-factly 'this union is ordained by God and we are INCREDIBLY happy'. Pastor dismissed Alyssa and I to talk privately about the incident and the state of our relationship amidst the allegations. I'm not sure what the other ladies were in for, but I could only imagine what I was about to experience.

When we entered my office, Alyssa only asked one thing. Why didn't you tell me about the hotel accommodations? I had to be honest, I just didn't know how nor how she would respond to it. To my amazement Alyssa said she understood and gave me a big hug. As I wiped the tears from her eyes, she began to ask me about my trip and the huge basket of flowers on my desk. I opened the door to

SELENA PEEKS, M.ED.

my office, and we spent the next few hours talking. After that day, I gained a weird respect for Marjorie. She literally held my professional career, my relationship and my reputation in her hands and yet she did the right thing.

Scene 6
I Want to Make Her My Wife

I'm so impressed with Alyssa I want to make her my wife, but before I can propose, I must meet her family. I wonder how she will react to my request since she's never even mentioned most of her family. I know she's incredibly close to her grandmother so maybe I can start there. I call her up. Alyssa, aren't you going to your family reunion in South Carolina this year? She replies yes excitedly, so I know that's my opening. Why don't I go with you, we can make it a mini vacation? Plus, it will give me an opportunity to meet grandma and the family. She said 'OK' but I could hear the hesitation in her voice. Then Alyssa asked, 'are you sure that's a good idea'? I reminded her that I have always and will continue to be a perfect gentleman. So, I suggested that she run it by her grandmother first. Secretly, I figured it would be the perfect opportunity to propose to her. I had my brother pick up the ring for me since it's so hard to be gone without either Marjorie or Alyssa noticing. Sister Marjorie can't keep a secret to save the children of Egypt so I couldn't let her know.

On the entire ride to the family reunion I could tell she was visibly nervous. She was rubbing her hands together and drying her palms on her knees. I tried to assure her I would be on my best behavior and try not to embarrass her. She smiled ever so sweetly but never said a word.

As we turn into the cul-de-sac, we could hear music blaring, the sounds of children laughing and playing, dominoes being slammed on the table and a whole lot of trash talk from the card tables. When we reached the house, there were huge barbeque grills going, turkey and fish being fried, and people playing beer pong in the front yard. I began to understand why Alyssa was so nervous about me coming. Not only does she have a colorful family, but there was alcohol and weed everywhere. I am a man of the cloth but I'm still human. I grab her hand and give her a nod to let her know that everything is ok. She quickly breathed a sigh of relief.

All of the family was so happy to see Alyssa that we barely made it into the house without a thousand hugs and kisses. Her grandmother's house was quaintly decorated like only a grandmother could. The sofa was covered in a plastic cover, pictures of all the kids and grandkids arranged on the wall grouped by families, and little statuettes (what-nots) everywhere. The smell of vanilla and real butter was permeating. I heard her grandmother calling for us from in the kitchen where she was baking her 7th cake from scratch. I didn't waste another second getting in there. I was so anxious I didn't wait on Alyssa to introduce me. I reached out to shake her grandmother's hand and she grabbed me and gave me a bug squeeze. Right then, I knew that I was in.

I was blushing and so nervous that I quickly blurted out 'will you be my wife'? She chuckled and said, I'm sure Alyssa would not like that very much baby. We both got a good laugh out of that one. I was about to show her the ring and ask if Alyssa would like it when Alyssa busted in to ask what so funny, and if I was flirting with her grandma. Beautiful, smart and with a sense of humor. I really hit the jackpot with this girl.

Her grandmother, the quick thinker that she is, told an old story about Alyssa's grandfather (bless his soul). He's been deceased for ten years now. I gave her a quick nod to thank her for not spoiling my surprise. Grandma just smiled ever so sweetly, and I knew instantly that I had her approval to ask Alyssa to be my wife. The rest of the weekend was filled with food, games and laughter. I was still a little anxious waiting for the perfect time to pop the question. But then it came, just like a scene out of the movies. With the arrival of her mom and cousin the timing just seemed right. After their hugs and greetings, I slipped the ring out of my pocket, dropped down on one knee and asked her to be my wife in front of a bunch of her friends and family. She started to cry just a little before she said yes. I was still impressed at the quality of that diamond. I had to pat myself on the back, Yeah, I did that!

Pastor was sure to announce our engagement during the next service and to remind me that Marjorie is still to be a constant fixture when we are alone.

We moved in together two months before our big day. That was the longest two months of my life. I remember walking in and catching her asleep on the coach looking like a goddess. I rubbed her hair careful not to wake her, but I really wanted to mount her like a wild beast. She must have felt me lusting because she jumped up out of sleep as if she had seen a ghost. I had to yell, it's me baby! Wow, feisty is no longer the word for her. Note to self, don't startle her it can become hazardous to one's health.

Scene 7
I Make Her My Wife

The entire wedding party has a room in our hotel, so we got little sleep that night. I was still a little groggy, but then I see her. Alyssa is simply beautiful as she walks down the aisle towards me. At that moment, it seemed that time stood still. I had to pinch myself to make sure I wasn't dreaming. I glanced over at my parents; mom is balling her eyes out. I then glance over at her parents and her mom is balling her eyes out as well. What's with women? Why do they cry when they are happy and when they are sad? My thoughts quickly go to nothing as my bride finally reaches me at the altar looking like an angel. I can hardly catch my breath. I reach out to take her hand and notice that mine is slightly trembling. The entire ceremony became a blur until I heard 'You may now kiss your bride'. You may now kiss the bride were the sweetest words of the entire day. I had the biggest, cheesiest grin on my face as I lean over to kiss her. I give her a sweet endearing kiss, after all our parents are watching…and crying. After that my thoughts quickly go to how long will it be before my wife and I can ditch our family and friends to start our honeymoon. I try to contain my excitement and stay in the moment. That was hard. I hope they have bubbles and not rice. Rice can get stuck in places that I am not trying remove in front of a room full of people. God, my wife is so beautiful, the ceremony was beautiful, our family and friends are all here and I can't be more thankful. I say a quick thank-you prayer and mentally get ready for the festivities. We are hurried to a waiting carriage to take us to the reception hall not too far from the church. As soon as we are in the carriage Sister Marjorie comes running towards us. This was odd, I thought. Alyssa looked a little panicked. When she reaches us, she stretches her hands and say congratulations you two. We both let out a sigh of relief. I was a bit confused as to why that gesture was such an emergency. We both dismissed it and prepared to enter the limo and enjoy the beginning to the rest of our lives together.

As we enter the DJ announces to everyone to please clear the dance floor… and now introducing Mr. and Mrs. Charleston and their first dance. Mrs. Charleston, I like the sound of that. Are you ready to show them how the Baptist preacher and his wife gets down, I asked Alyssa? She just smiles at me lovingly and nods. Alyssa has been unusually quiet since we left the church. Today has been long. Our first dance. We twirl and grind to 'Here and Now' by Big Luther as I gaze into her eyes. I notice a small tear roll down her cheek. I realize that she is totally into this moment with me, and I'm in love all over again. We are one and it feels amazing. Then Marjorie strolls over and ask to cut in. My wife always being a gracious host quickly agrees. I'm screaming 'NO' in my head at this moment. Dang can she be more of a pester? Hi Marjorie, did you enjoy the ceremony? I ask. She says, yes but I would enjoy your brother more. Then it hits me. I asks her if I can introduce them, I will be able to enjoy my wife uninterrupted. Marjorie happily agrees. So, I race over to whisper in his ear to take Marjorie off my hands. It's just one problem, he himself is married. I ask him to entertain her so I can enjoy my new wife. Is that too much to ask? Then I notice Alyssa giving me that look again on what's supposed to be one of the happiest days of our lives. I felt two inches small. My brother came to my rescue to keep Marjorie out of my face. He's always a trooper and one of my biggest supporters. Now I can concentrate on consummating this marriage.

Scene 8
The Honeymoon

We made it out of the reception relatively intact, even though it took us more than 20 minutes to say goodbye to everyone for the fiftieth time. I couldn't believe it, but both our phones were ringing before we got to the airport. We both looked at each other and seemingly on queue we cut the phones off. Of course, the Atlanta airport is always a bother, so we decide to make-out in the counter to calm our frayed nerves and help pass the time. Our plane is departing on time. Oh yeah, oh yeah! Time to consummate this marriage. As we stepped off the plane, it seemed that time stopped. To say it was magical was an understatement. When we made it out of the airport of Honolulu we were greeted with leis and grass skirts. The sounds of the locals playing the drums and the magnificent aroma of smoked pork in the air. We made it to our waiting car to take us to the resort on the island of Oahu on the way to Waikiki, Hawaii. It was even more breathtaking than I expected. The staff was waiting on us to arrive with a 'Just Married' sign with our names and wedding date on it. They greeted us and grabbed our luggage before leading us through the lobby with marble floors. There was a glass of champagne and chocolates waiting for us at the counter.

After we checked in, we were given our itinerary and lead to our suite all the while being serenaded by some local musicians. Our suite was decorated immaculately. There was a stunning view of the ocean. The staff put a trail of rose petals from the door leading to the heart shaped jacuzzi tub located right off from the bedroom. There was also a single red rose on the bed with champagne and fruit on the nightstand. This place is just full of surprises I told Alyssa. She just giggled and told me the rose petals were her idea. Wow, my wife. I like the sound of that. Yes, my WIFE is amazing. I tipped the staff and hurried them out of the room so we could check out the suite and each other. We made an exception to our vow of purity and poured ourselves a second glass of champagne. Then we proceeded to the heart shaped jacuzzi to run a bath. After a 10 and half hour flight, a relaxing bath in the jacuzzi is just what the doctor ordered. Watching Alyssa undress, I couldn't contain my excitement. I took her into my arms, toted her to the bathroom and sat her on the countertop where I begin to enjoy her sweet nectar for the first time. As I began to kiss her in that special spot, she screamed with excitement. I lifted her brown sugar body into the tub and took my place between her legs with the back of my head pressed firmly against her supple breast. She lifted the sponge to squeeze the warm water over my head and back while she gently stroked my manhood until I erupted. I quickly spun around and without a second thought Alyssa was straddling me like a baby. She bucked and gyrated in my lap like a wild pony. I admit it turned me on so much that I came two more times before she was ready to take our first break. I toted her to the bed and dried and moisturized her silky skin just hard enough to loosen up her tensed muscles. As she dozed off, I climbed in the bed behind her. I think I must have held her for 20 minutes before dozing off myself. When we woke up around 2:00 am, we went for round two. Everything seemed to come so naturally. I didn't have to tell her anything, she amazingly knew everything that I liked. She even had a few tricks of her own. I liked them too. This girl is perfect. Right then the phone in our room started to ring. It rang for about seven minutes until we were forced to answer. The voice on the other end hit me like a ton of bricks. Oh shit, it's Marjorie! I knew Alyssa wouldn't be happy. I noticed how my wife was looking at me. I asked Marjorie what she needed and tried to rush her off the phone before Alyssa had a conniption. Alyssa is a very smart woman; she immediately noticed the look on my face immediately. I had to tell her who was calling and take the question and answer session like a man, although it would cost me some loving and conversation later.

Scene 9
Back to Reality

We put the 'do not disturb' line on the phone and the door. We enjoyed four more glorious days in paradise just the two of us. As we were packing to come back home, reality set in. These next few weeks may not be so glamourous. As expected, the entourage of our wedding party met us at the airport. They were all asking questions about the trip in succession without us being able to answer the first one. Who really wants to talk about making love to your wife all day long in front of your parents? Not this guy right here. It was an hour before we got out of the airport. Then I got the dreaded phone call, it was Marjorie again. I instantly sent her to voicemail and listened to the message when I got in the car. The message said I was immediately needed at the church. Great, just back from a fabulous week and now this. What now? I drop Alyssa off at our home hustle back to the church to see what's the emergency. It seems that someone has forgot to pay the taxes for two years. Two years, no accident. I'm thinking, REALLY? Someone is stealing from the church. Jamal is Bishop's oldest brother and the church treasurer. I co-signed those checks myself. How do I tell Bishop that his brother is stealing from the House of God? I man up and just tell him. The reaction was not good, after all that is his family. I could see the hurt in his eyes. He almost came to tears. I'm sure he cried later that night. The hard part was still yet to come, deciding what to do about it.

The elders of the church had a meeting. After a little forensic accounting, we concluded that about 60 thousand dollars was taken over the last two years. Who knows exactly how much was taken? The decision was made to have Jamal pay back the money via payment plan, a two-month suspension from the board and 60 hours of community service to the orphanage. We all decided that it would be best for Pastor to deliver the news since they are family.

I heard he didn't take the news well. As a matter of fact, Jamal felt that the punishment didn't fit the crime although he could've been arrested. He reluctantly agreed to the request, but it was obvious that he didn't like it one bit especially if I had a say in it.

The meeting went a little longer than expected and the Mrs. must be really missing her homey, lover friend by now. This is the third phone call. I'll stop by Kroger and pick up her some flowers and frozen yogurt. Maybe she won't be so irritated with me and we can have honeymoon part two. YEAH!

Instead she tells me she's taken a volunteer assignment down at the Union Mission and she has to get up early, so she is going to sleep now. How can I compete with that? She falls fast asleep; I say a quick prayer and kiss her on forehead.

Scene 10
Disappointment

I rush through the self-checkout without even bagging my purchase. I am off to see my queen. As I arrive, I notice a strange vehicle in the driveway. I pull the gun out of the glove compartment and quietly make my way around to the back of the house to see what's going on. As I approach the backyard, I can hear angry voices. I listen a little longer and I realize it's Marjorie. What is she doing here and why wasn't she present for the meeting tonight at the sanctuary?

I tap lightly before entering. Alyssa immediately runs to my arms and give me a big squeeze. I don't know what just happened, but it clearly upset her. I asked Sister Marjorie 'to what do we owe the pleasure?' She simply said she wanted to come check on Alyssa since she knew I had to attend an emergency meeting. I thanked her and told her that her gesture was thoughtful, but we've had a long day and would like to get some rest. Just as if I had said nothing, Sister Marjorie asked how did the meeting go? This lady cannot take a hint. So, I grab her by the hand and her purse with my other hand and lead her to the front door while telling her she will get a full explanation tomorrow to document in the church records. My second mind was screaming had you been doing your job and not over here harassing my wife, you would know how the meeting went. Goodnight Sister Marjorie, before she could get the next sentence out, I repeated 'GOODNIGHT! Sister Marjorie' forcefully. She finally got the message and scurried off.

    I turned around to talk to Alyssa about what happened, but she just walked up the stairs as if she had heard the worst news of her life. What's even more torturous is that she won't even talk to me about it. Maybe after a good hot bath, she will be ready to talk about it. I rush to the bathroom and tell her I have just the remedy for her. I start the water in the tub and rush back out to the car to get her flowers and frozen yogurt. By the time I come back, Alyssa is fast asleep. Wow, another missed opportunity. I'm not giving up though. I cuddle up next to her and follow suit, but I see papers from The Innocence Project. Is there someone that she feels was wrongfully convicted? I will deal with it tomorrow. Of course, the Bible tells us that 'Joy cometh in the morning'.

Scene 11
The Secret Meetings

Sunday's services went off without a hitch, or so I thought. I sat in my office and ran over the books once more to see if everything was accounted for. As usual, the money from Deacon Jamal is not here. Something in my spirit was telling me something was amiss. Not only was his scheduled payment missing, but the entire entry from the Mother Board's bake sell mysteriously disappeared. Just trifling, I thought. I must talk to Pastor about this. I know he is in another meeting, but this is important. I make my way passed the sisters, the kids, Pastor's wife and the Deacon firing squad. When I enter the room, I see most of the Board surrounding Pastor and the air is so thick you can cut it with a knife. A board meeting and I wasn't invited, I thought? Something is up. I quickly apologize for being late to the meeting, and eerily there was no response. An awkward silence fell upon the room. I knew then that I was intentionally left out of this meeting. This made me think somehow the information that I was about to give pastor about Jamal would be unwanted at this moment. I just excused myself to find Alyssa as fast I could.

As I pass by the pastor's secretary, I overhear Marjorie telling another sister that this is not the first of such secret meeting and inquiring if she should tell me or not. Am I losing my mind or are they hiding something from me? I would be lying if I said that I do not feel betrayed. I'm pastor's right hand, confidant and friend. Maybe I'm just overreacting. Just then, Marjorie popped out of her office and asked if we could talk. I could tell that she was visibly nervous, so I just told her to spill it. She began by saying that she would never intentionally hide anything from me. She went on to explain that she thought I was being left out because I was busy since Alyssa and I were just returning from our honeymoon. I asked her how long have these meetings been taking place? To my surprise, she replied since the week before we left for our honeymoon. I told Marjorie thank you and assured her that this conversation would stay between us.

I will have to address my concerns with pastor later but not in front of the Elders that have more letters behind their names that are in the first half of the alphabet. I found Alyssa in the main sanctuary dutifully placing Bibles behind each seat and making sure that the used gum was removed from beneath. I quietly explained to her what I observed in the Pastor's study and the information that I received from Marjorie (to which I swore her to secrecy). I didn't expect her to do about it, but I felt compelled to tell her. Needless to say, she was just as surprised and I was. She gave me a huge hug and told me that we would pray for discernment when we got home. I swear this girl always know exactly what to say. I'm so blessed to have her.

Apparently, Alyssa had begun holding her own secret Book Club meetings while waiting on me to get out of our weekly Elder meetings. I had no idea that she was mentoring young ladies on dating and the sanctity of marriage. Word travels fast, but it only serves to increase my status in the church and catapult me toward a more senior role. The Bonnie to my Clyde. I smiled to myself and walked my queen out to the car.

Scene 12

The Showdown

I processed my feelings for weeks before confronting Pastor. I tried to convince myself that I was being overly sensitive. I looked for Alyssa in the sanctuary, but she was not there. I looked for her in the Women's Lounge she wasn't there either. I finally found her in the basement with the Book Club and there was a new member that seems to have been battered. Alyssa turned to meeting over to Marjorie for a few minutes so we could talk. After having one last conversation with Alyssa, I make my way to Pastor's study to have one of the worst conversations of my life. Surprisingly, he greeted me with a hug and the biggest smile. Maybe my apprehension had been all for not. I let out a huge sigh of relief and a huge smile came upon my face. I took off my sports coat and sat down in the huge leather lazy boy recliner right beside pastor. I was telling myself to stop grinning so hard, I guess I really didn't realize how much I wanted and valued his approval. Just then, Pastor comes from behind his desk. The look on his face let me know that all the previous pleasantries were just a front. Quickly my smile turned upside down. I tried to brace myself for what was coming next. I begin to perspire a little as I try to focus on what I originally came here for. I was so nervous in that moment that I almost forgot that I called the meeting. As he circled me like a buzzard stalking his prey, I quickly stood up to level the playing field. I tried to explain that I'm sure that the recent events were mainly coincidences, but I thought I should discuss it with him anyway. I noticed his facial expressions so I tried not to give him any eye contact so that I could maintain my composure. I started off by saying, I'm sure I'm overreacting, to which he wasted no time interrupting me and asking why I would waste his time. Why is he being so defensive when he doesn't even know what my concerns are, I thought. I took a deep breath and begin to rattle off my list of concerns that I had prepared with Alyssa the week before. I started off my telling Pastor that Jamal had not returned the money that he had stolen, and I also alerted him to the additional monies that were missing from the Mother Board bake sale. There was an awkward silence in the room. It seemed like forever, I'm sure it was only about 3 minutes. Pastor startled me by slamming his hand on his desk. He let out a long sigh, straightened his tie, and gave me the most piercing look before he begins to speak.' Son, do you know what it takes to run a church'? No sir, I responded. 'Do you know how many lives can be destroyed when you think selfishly?' he asked. Before I could respond he said, there are two thousand people that count on us to give them hope every week, people who need to believe that this church is flawless, that WE are flawless. Do you understand what I am telling you son? To which I replied, perfectly. I realized that Pastor had known all along. That's what all the secret meetings were about. I was the only one that wasn't informed. Never in all my years had I felt so crushed and deceived. I begin to wonder if anything he ever told me was true. I got out of that office as fast as I could without mumbling another word. It is clear what I must do now.

Scene 13

The Following Year

Alyssa and I had a wonderful time celebrating our first anniversary in Acapulco, even if Marjorie called us 20 times. Marjorie can become quite needy when we are away. The week away was a much-needed distraction after the world wind year we've had. A year of growing and learning how to support each other all while starting a new church can be incredibly stressful. We are really in our season of expansion. God is blessing us at every turn. The new church is simply beautiful, more than I could ever hope for. We can seat 500 in the main sanctuary, and another 100 in the overflow room that also doubles as conference space. The seats are adorned in a beautiful burgundy crushed velvet. There are four classrooms that seats 30 equipped with projectors. We have a childcare for use during service in the north wing and a bookstore/library in the south wing. Marjorie's office is right off from my study in the east wing. That makes it easy for us to handle business late into the evening. My wife's study is in the east wing. Downstairs in the basement we have a coffee bar and a room that houses unperishable food and clothing for the needy. We have a full-service childcare facility and preschool to the right of the church all sitting on two and a half acres. This year was trying, from the misunderstandings with Alyssa to the knockdown, drag-outs with half of the members. My leaving caused a big division in the church. Half of the members chose to stay with Pastor and the other half chose to rebuild with us. Someone even left dead animals on the church steps. It always seemed to happen when Marjorie was there alone. She decided to come with us to become my Executive Secretary. Pastor was not happy about that at all. He even called to tell me that I was leading her and other souls to hell. I won't lie, it hurt the first few times. I became numb to the effects after the fifth time. He also told me that he would block my membership to the Southeast Conference of the Apostolic International Convention (the governing body for our denomination). This would certainly limit my ability to become part of certain well-known TV and world-wide missionary ministries. Alyssa forced me to apply to the conference numerous times and on the 6th attempt, I was finally accepted. No doubt this was one cause of the second division of the congregation. After that became known, the members who had been on the fence about leaving Pastor joined our new church. Shortly after that mass exodus, our church and daycare began to get vandalized. For four full months our congregation endured defacing of the sanctuary with paint, destruction of the trees and landscaping, mounds of dirt in the parking lot, numerous complaints to the fire inspector, and the windows being broken out in the daycare. Alyssa has been my uber strong rock throughout this whole ordeal. Lords knows I needed. She never let me give up, even when my confidence was in the toilet. Now I marvel at how we weathered the ups and downs over this past year and still manage to still be very much in love.

Scene 14
Perseverance Pays Off

It was just an ordinary Saturday, but Alyssa asked me if she could move the Book Club to our home in the basement. Maybe the government had cut back on the time they could be there. Sometimes they can go pretty late in the night, I am out on my terrace enjoying the beautiful sounds of nature and putting the final touches on my sermon for Sunday when I hear Alyssa running and screaming. The scream was so loud that I jumped up and wasted the pitcher of strawberry lemonade I was enjoying trying to see what the commotion was about. Once the shock from the ice and berries wore off, I noticed that Marjorie and Alyssa were running toward me waving an envelope in the air as if they were bringing in a 757. It looked like a PCH commercial. Marjorie had received a letter from the Southeast Conference of the Apostolic International Convention. Of course, Marjorie had already opened it and claims she did 80 on the freeway to get it to us. Alyssa became overcome with emotion as she was reading the letter. After about five minutes Alyssa calmed down enough to tell me what all of the hoopla was about. I had been asked to be the Keynote Speaker for the upcoming convention. That is a huge deal considering I had just been accepted as a member and I am the youngest minister to ever embark on such a challenge. I couldn't contain my excitement, so I broke out in my Holy dance right there on the terrace. I didn't care if the neighbors saw me. After a few congratulatory hugs from Alyssa, Marjorie and I immediately went to work on my sermon for the convention. Marjorie was incredibly attentive, researching topics and the Greek and Latin interpretations of certain books of the Bible. She even researched the meaning of certain hieroglyphics. I think it must have been 9 hours before we even took a break. Alyssa came in to bring us dinner. At that time Marjorie was leaning over my shoulder to proofread the closing of my sermon for the conference. I looked up to say thank you and noticed a strange look on her face. Marjorie was having what is now known as a 'wardrobe malfunction'. Wow, this looks horrible, but I had nothing to do with this. She trusts me, right? I can just explain it to her later, I hope. However, I realize I may be getting the silent treatment tonight and little to no loving. After two more hours of working I decided it was time for bed. Just when I was about to go into the bedroom, I realized that Alyssa had locked the bedroom door. That's when I realized, I should have explained earlier, maybe this could've been avoided. I banged on the door and begged for Alyssa to let me in so we could talk. Once she finally let me in, it still took a few hours for me to convince her to let me explain. She said ok, but the look on her face made me believe that she was still doubtful. I don't know why, but I feel like this situation is not over.

Scene 15
Southeast Conference of the Apostolic International Convention

The next few weeks went off without a hitch, although I was still on pins and needles from the wardrobe incident with Marjorie. I paced back and forth in my study, I prayed, I fasted and paced some more. Marjorie came over Monday to help me put the finishing touches on my sermon because we were leaving the next day. She also made sure Alyssa had the perfect outfit to compliment mine. Marjorie emerged in the study with two of Alyssa's dresses to see which one I would prefer. Both outfits were equally elegant, but the second one hugged all of her vivacious curves, yes, yes Marjorie number two. It was only when 'Pastor, Pastor' repeatedly that I snapped out of my daydream I quickly wiped the little drool from my mouth and shouted, 'number two Marjorie, that will be all'. I didn't realize the brashness in my voice. I could see a small smirk on Marjorie's face as if she could read my mind. We arrived at the airport the next day about an hour and a half early. Another flight had to be cancelled for mechanical issues, so our flight filled up quickly. We were one of the first passengers to be asked to be moved to first class. We accepted of course. I can tell you that first class is a very different experience from coach by far. Everything was going perfectly. It was the first time in a long time that Marjorie and Alyssa were genuinely enjoying each other's company, so I was careful to stay out of the way. I grabbed a quick nap and the next thing I know we were landing in New Orleans. The city is just filled with culture. The aroma of southern cuisines was in the air. It seemed that street musicians were on every corner. I was simply blown away by the amazing saxophone players. Jazz, jazz and more jazz. There it is again, that feeling that everything is 'too perfect'. I have to get my heads out of the clouds and focus at the task at hand. I'm the keynote speaker at this conference. I can make it or break it for the generation of young pastors coming after me. I cannot mess this up. As we shuffle through the airport, we see our chauffer waiting for us, wow I could get used to this. Marjorie wasted no time introducing herself to our driver. I think she almost forgot she was only there because of us. I took the intuitive to let him know we were the guests he was there to pick up. I could tell he was relieved; I think the sign gave it away. I should probably talk to Marjorie about her approach, umm…yeah it will have to wait. We stayed in the best hotel on Canal Street. but my mind's eye couldn't wait to get Alyssa back to the room. The married bed is undefiled, right? I'm still a man. After that night of passion with Alyssa, all my inhibitions left, and I was able to go on to deliver one the best sermon of my life. Standing ovations, I became the great young hope. Marjorie wasted no time to jumping my arms after the sermon, no…she literally jumped in my arms. All I could think about was back to the couch I go. I just got out of the dog-house. I know how it looks, in mid thought all of the other elders made sure to invite as a keynote speaker to next year's session. I don't think flowers will do it this time. Alyssa is a trooper, but I can tell these excursions with Marjorie are starting to wear on her. She doesn't deserve to feel like this. I can fix it. They had a good flight, ok, I think I can fix it. Marjorie wasn't able to sit with us on the flight home, she made the biggest scene at the airport. I was secretly happy. Great, I have a chance to talk to Alyssa. I think she understood but she offered no resistance. That worried me, maybe she was tired.

Scene 16
I Came, I Saw, I Conquered...

Coming back from the SCAIC, I was riding the biggest emotional high I've ever experienced in my adult life. Well, besides that moment I saw my beautiful bride and realized she would be all mine forever. I swear every traffic light stopped for me. I thought to myself, I'm the man, oh yeah, I'm the man. Alyssa told our family and friends that I 'killed it' at the conference, so my welcome home reception was phenomenal. The local fireman met us at the airport and led the convoy all the way to my neighborhood where our family and friends waited. Wow, this girl is amazing. I think I fell in love with Alyssa all over again that day. When we got home, I kissed her parents and my grandmother goodnight. Even in all of the excitement of the day, I started to get an uneasy feeling, something just wasn't quite right. Alyssa was being her sweet, gentle self. She was wearing my favorite night gown, the one that I bought her for Valentines' Day. Something was still amidst. Maybe I'm just being hypersensitive after all of the exhilaration of the conference. I had to admit that I was still on edge from our last encounter with Marjorie; yet I was secretly hoping that the great experience from the conference would make all things right. I climbed into bed next to my beautiful wife, surprisingly she was waiting for me. Wow, this feels like the old days (when she actually liked me). I can tell at this moment she is proud that I am her husband. That's the best feeling in the world. She sat up, grabbed me by necktie and pulled me close to her. She whispered 'Hercules, Hercules' in my ear before sticking her tongue in that left one. I could smell Aqua Di Gio on her neck. Maybe, she put on one of my coats? She climbed on top of me and kissed my neck gently. While looking me in my eyes, she pushed me inside of her. She bucked and gyrated for what seemed like an eternity. I loved every minute of it. I remember this stallion, time saddle to up. It seemed that time was standing still. Nothing and no one else mattered. When we were done, I could tell she was satisfied, that purr before she fell asleep solidified it. Yeah, I'm the man. I awoke after several hours to Alyssa licking my chest. This is different, but I like it. Oh, Alyssa, Alyssa, Alyssa. This went on for several weeks. I was optimistic that the awkwardness between us has surpassed. It did for a while. I'm not one for coincident either, so I can understand Alyssa's lack of faith in me. I vowed then to win her trust back.

Scene 17
I Can Make Her Love Me…Again

After the conference, the speaking engagements and conference invitations skyrocketed. I made sure Alyssa was involved in every decision. She ultimately decided which ones to take and how often I should be on the road. After all, I am trying to convince her that I can be a Pastor and a father, wink. The very first one that we accepted was in Jacksonville, Fl to give a seminar to some up and coming Pastors. We touched on subjects such as handling temptations when you are single, handling celibacy while dating, and the balance of power when leading in the black church. These are very sensitive subjects, but I was not afraid. Alyssa was ecstatic about the idea. She smiled and tilted her head so lovingly. I missed that smile and the way she looked into my eyes as we put the finishing touches on the lesson. As a matter of fact, I think she did more research on my sermon than Marjorie. It was nice, to have my partner in crime again. We decided that Marjorie we didn't need Marjorie to come along on this trip since Marjorie had such an indebt knowledge of the lesson. Marjorie also gave her strict instructions on when are appropriate times and reasons to all. Everything else, my brother and co-pastor can handle until I return. Surprisingly, Marjorie took the news very well and scurried off to break the news to my brother Daryl. I have a feeling he will be fielding most of calls while I am gone. The hosting church had a car waiting for us when we arrived. The deacons made sure we made it to our hotel and grabbed a bite to eat before getting to the business at hand. This engagement is a rather lucrative one and if we decided to stay for the Sunday service, they will take up a special offering just for us. I think I will pass on that one and return to my own church, not without discussing it with Alyssa first. Friday night and Saturday went great. The new pastors were attentive and engaged. They were also eager to ask Alyssa frank questions about our dating life. She enjoyed every minute of the spotlight. Once we got back to our hotel, Alyssa surprised me with candles, soft music and a quiet dinner for two. I showed her my gratitude by running her a nice bubble bath and giving her a back rub in the tub. I know what I'm having for dessert. Now, this is how things should be between us. We've already made it six years. Now if we can pass the "seven-year itch" I'll believe in our forever again.

Scene 18
I'm Feeling the Love Again

On the way to breakfast the song 'Matrimony' by Wale and Usher came on the radio. Alyssa gave me that look again. You know the 'I want you so bad *right* now' look. In that moment it seemed that every lyric of the song described our relationship. 'Nothing is sacred anymore, Wale wailed. I had to disagree with him on this point. My faith in God is sacred and so is my relationship to Alyssa. My calling is to love her like Christ loves the church. Somewhere along the way, I either forgot that point or took her for granted. Maybe a little bit of both. My personal vow is to make her a priority and to make sure that she knows it. I never want to see those sad, empty eyes again. That look of pure despair was devastating to me. The point when I knew she gave up on me crushed me to my very soul. (*Lyrics from the song still chiming*). 'I plan to do it better yo'! Yes, this has to be divine intervention. Every verse of this song is resonating with me. Alyssa is bobbing to the music too as she flashes me a slight smile. Then she puts her hand on my knee, WOOO! Stay focus, the yellow lines are there for a reason.

On the way back to the hotel from breakfast the song playing is non-other than John Legend's 'All of Me'. Can this get any better? Again, this song is saying everything I'm thinking and feeling right now. She is my end and beginning on this Earth, her imperfections are perfect. John Legend is a lyrical genius. I don't want to ever imagine life without her. I know she will always be there for me and me only, as long as I don't hurt her again. Once we reach the hotel, I open the door for my queen. She made sure she brushed up against me as she exited the vehicle and gave me a nice little squeeze on the rear end. Woo-hoo! That made me feel like I'd just won a gold medal. I can't wait to get her back to the room. I want to surprise her with something, but we are walking hand in hand and I don't want to spoil this moment. I got to figure out how to make this happen and quickly. Just then the phone rings and it's Marjorie calling for the third time (it's not quite 10:00 am). What can it be now? Now I see why Alyssa gets annoyed. Wait, this can be my chance to surprise her once more before we leave. My mind is racing a mile a minute. I just want to be her 'knight in shining armor' again. I can't believe how corny I sound to myself right now. I tell Alyssa to go ahead so I can take the call with Marjorie. I'm sure she doesn't appreciate that, but she will.

Scene 19
It's Showtime

As Alyssa walks to the elevator the bellman catches up with her and present her with the passion colored roses that I ordered the night before. (By the way- I did not know that Passion-colored roses exists). Those put the biggest smile on her face. At that moment Marjorie rings my phone again. I tell Alyssa that Marjorie has called six times so I should probably take this. It will only take a moment I said. She was still admiring the unique roses she probably didn't care if I had jumped in a lake. I hurry in the opposite direction to take the call from Marjorie.

Once I was out of earshot of Alyssa, I screamed to Marjorie that I really needed her before her motor mouth could unleash on me. To my surprise, she replied anything Pastor and listened intently. I told her I needed chocolate covered strawberries, sparkling cider, red rose petals, lavender candles, and one-hour deep tissue massage and a bracelet stat. I informed her that the Spa has just opened and if she hurries, Alyssa can get in now. Oh, that's easy. I asked her to repeat it back to me because she answered too fast. Marjorie played back my list of requests like a tape recorder. Don't worry Pastor, I got you she said. I must've had a humongous grin on my face because when I turned around to go the elevator the front desk staff applauded and congratulated me. I nodded and rushed back to my queen.

I am clumsily rushing back to the elevator. Making her wait especially when it comes to Marjorie annoys the hell out of her and I will not spoil this moment. I asked Alyssa would she do me the honor of allowing me to spoil her today. 'If you insist', she replied jokingly. I tell her that there is a massage with her name on it, she flashes me a half smile and then the front desk motioned for Alyssa to come over. I accompanied her, grabbed her roses and watched her wave on her way to the Spa with an extra twitch in those hips. I wish I knew what she was thinking right now. Our situation is still delicate right now. I have just under 50 minutes to gather everything and set the stage for my surprise. As soon as she was safely out of sight, I alerted the manager of the plan.

Just then she walked in and caught me doing my famous non-dancing. My moves remind you of an ostrich walking on hot coals as Alyssa described it. She almost choked she was laughing so hard. Wow... I can still make her laugh. I have a chance to make this day special and let her know how sorry I am for not showing her know how much she truly means to me. I guess like most men, I got caught up in my success and believed she would always be there.

Just then there was a knock at the door. There stood an incredibly young staff member rubbing his hands looking nervous. He told Alyssa she was urgently needed at the front desk. She turned around and nodded with a look of worry on her face, I nodded back to say 'OK' and she ran to the elevator. As soon as the elevator doors closed, the catering staff rushed around the corner with two carts carrying the goodies that I requested. I could barely wait until the hotel doors closed. I hurried to get the candles lit, the rose petals on the floor and to take one last peek at the bracelet. It is a beautiful bracelet if I do say so myself. Marjorie hit a home run as usual. She even managed to buy Alyssa a negligée. The staff was excited to play along as well.

After about 15 minutes, the receptionist phones the room to let me know that Alyssa is on her way back and she was not happy. The catering staff was barely out of the room when I heard the ding of the elevator. I quickly cut off the lights in the front room of the suite. Alyssa bursts into the room agitated about the bogus call to the front desk and equally frustrated by the darkness. 'Why is it so dark in here', she asks? I flick on the first lamp and respond, 'so you can follow me on this highway of love'. I know it was corny, but that is the best I could come up with in that moment. Me, an excellent orator lost for words. Alyssa does that to me.

As Alyssa enters the bedroom area, she notices the different color rose petals on the floor. She flashes a huge grin across her face and started to giggle uncontrollably. Ah ha, I got her. I yelled hey Google, play love her. I grabbed her quickly and pulled her close to me. We stood in the middle of the room holding each other and swaying from side to side. I caressed her face while I searched her eyes for the look I hadn't seen in so long. And there it was, the look of adoration. Through the pain and aggravation that soft, kind, loving look was back. In my head I was standing on the table beating my chest like Tarzan, yeah that's the primitive me.

Scene 20
If It Not for Bad Luck...

I was so full of emotion when we got back from our trip. I decided to by the office to debrief with the senior pastors. Alyssa wanted to get dropped off at her mom's house. I was praying she was telling her that I could remove that huge body pillow in the middle of our bed. I'm feeling pretty confident right now.

Alyssa called me all excited once she reached her parents house. She wanted to let me know that they will be hanging out at the mall and going to dinner afterwards. She started giggling and told me she wanted to talk to me later. That gives me at least five hours at the church. One my way there my phone started to ring uncontrollably. It was Marjorie again, I decided not to answer since I was only seven minutes from the church. I noticed a lot of firetrucks and EMTs as I turned down the street toward the church. I wasn't able to get through, so I called Marjorie to see what all of the commotion was about. She knows everything about everyone she encounters. This time the someone is us. The church is on fire. I called Alyssa and left a message. I was glad she didn't answer because I didn't have any specifics for her. They first responders weren't letting anyone through.

After some convincing and throwing my name around, I was finally about to get through the barricade to access the damage. The entire church was engulfed in flames. I couldn't believe it. Marjorie assured me that everyone had gotten out with little more that smoke inhalation. Three people were headed to the emergency room. I just stood there feeling helpless, wondering how this could've happened. How was I not able to protect my flock? I felt awful for being away while all of this had taken place. Before I knew it, the tears started streaming. I didn't even realize it until Marjorie started to embrace me. I just collapsed in her arms.

Alyssa and her mom pulled up just as the snot started run. I was trying so hard to catch my breath that I didn't notice her at first. Marjorie tapped me on shoulder to let me know she had arrived. Alyssa was not looking too pleased to see the embrace between Marjorie and me. I really needed her at the exact moment, so I didn't care. I scurried over to Alyssa and placed my head in her bosom and wept like a baby. Her mother suggested that we go home and wait on the report from the fire marshals.

Her mother quizzed me with the questions that I know Alyssa was thinking of asking. That was the longest ride home. I could barely answer through my tears. Plus, I didn't want her to think I was lying about my intentions with Marjorie by stuttering. Momma Rose lit into me like I had stolen her last five dollars and ate the last piece of pie. I can only hope Alyssa gives me time to lick some of my wombs when her mom leaves before she inflicts further pain. I'm already feeling defeated from watching the last three years of my life goes up in flames. With all of the mishaps lately, I'm no longer sure it this is my calling. Lord, I need your help right now.

My faith had completely been shattered. As I was laying on the couch in Alyssa's lap thinking of giving up, I realized that God had not ever forsaken me (although I felt that way at that moment). I started to pray, and the tears came streaming yet again. Alyssa being the dutiful wife that she is was trying her best to console me. She prayed with me, she prayed for me and she cried with me. I had to let her know how much this moment with her is helping me hold on to my faith. She looked at me and said maybe I can help you feel just a little bit better. She grabbed my hand and put it on her belly and rubbed it back and forth. The stay of mind I was in I thought she wanted to make love. It turns out, while she was at her mom's house, she had taken a pregnancy test and it was positive. Hearing the news that I about to bring a new life in the world with my queen made all the emotions of the day worth it. That surely restored my faith and I think I can fight again. Thank you, Lord.

Scene 21

Where There Is Smoke, There Is Fire

It took over five weeks of investigation for us to get the report for the fire department. Of course, without that report, we could file an insurance claim. Once the smoke finally dissipated (literally), we were alerted that the church had been torched purposely. I was extremely surprised and a bit disappointed. Had I not seen the reports from the fire inspectors myself, I would not have believed it. While I was busy being worried about rebuilding, we had bigger problems. There were legal implications surrounding the fire. Because this had been our second property fire, the senior leadership of our church became immediate suspects. The first fire was contained to the outside of the church, so the investigation had concluded that maybe it was vandals and the insurance company paid quickly. This fire was totally different. Not only had it been started on the inside of the building, it had completely engulfed the structure.

The fire inspector alerted the local police departments of our respective locales. Arson and be handled by the regular authorities, but because we were suspected of trying to commit insurance fraud in the amount of 1.5 million dollars, the GBI was also called. We were all questioned repeatedly by both agencies. Our cellphones and house phones records were subpoenaed. Maybe even tapped. The Elders were asked to surrender their financial records and tax returns. Some of us were being followed by the GBI for months. This was especially difficult on Alyssa because she was pregnant and feeling like I may be unfaithful to her.

We were renting a store front to hold services. I remember seeing new faces attending our Friday night and Sunday services. The detectives were not even trying to conceal their presence. Me being the senior pastor, Alyssa and I had the most scrutiny. Our family and friends we questioned about our relationship and finances. An officer even met us at our home after a prenatal appointment 'to ask a few more questions'. I never knew the people sworn to 'protect and serve' used so many intimidation tactics. This went on for more than a year, but finally the insurance company paid our claim and quickly cancelled our policy. However, the local authorities informed us that investigation was still open and we should let them know if we plan to leave the area. I was personally offended that were still being treated as criminals.

Once the check finally clears it time to kick into overdrive to get this building back up. I must've sent at least five hours a day on the phone with Marjorie, Daryl and the contractor every day for four months while trying to help Alyssa with our new baby girl.

Scene 22
The Aftermath

As it came closer to our grand reopening Marjorie and I were making frequent trips to the new sanctuary and conducting phone meetings with the Elders. I could feel the tension rising between Alyssa and me. Some days we didn't even talk unless it was about the baby. Physical contact was almost nonexistent. As frustrated as I were, I tried not to stress her about it. I know she was having a hard time dealing being a new mother and me being away so much. But I could definitely see a change in her. How can I lead a flock if my home is in disarray?

I know we still love each other so we begin going to counseling. We went to see a Christian counselor once a week together and every other we separately. I was totally committed to doing the assignments and being mentally invested when I do.

Counseling doesn't seem to be working anymore. Alyssa and I are arguing more than ever nowadays. Heading to the sanctuary is now a welcomed release instead of work. My little Princess is the only thing that is good about home, so I unconsciously spend more and more time at my office. I still came home and spent time with my daughter and fixed Alyssa dinner. I made sure she had a body massage once a week; but every time I got on the phone with Marjorie the conversation slightly veered from church business there was going to be hell to pay. I was getting no sleep and no loving. I was running on fumes by the time we reopened.

We were all working until the very last 12 hours until opening day. Alyssa stayed home with the baby. I didn't feel so bad for staying late because her mom came to stay with her. I thought for sure Alyssa and the baby would be sleeping by the time I got home. But they both were in the living room waiting. She asked me if everything was ready to go. I got that jittery feeling again, and we stayed up and talked to the early morning hours with the baby between us. I have to admit, I missed that closeness with her.

When we woke up the next morning, Alyssa surprised me with breakfast and some lovemaking. I was so excited; I could hardly contain myself. Alyssa wanted to take the baby and go ahead of me so she can take a peek at the finished product before the rest of the parishioners got there. Although, that was unusual for us, I agreed so I can get mentally ready for service.

When I got there, I was surprised to see Alyssa wasn't in her normal seat and her mom had Princess. I didn't think that was such a big deal. I was still riding the high from last night and this morning. I made a B-line to my office to start my Sunday ritual of prayer and meditation and to review my sermon one more time. I was having a weird feeling like it was my first sermon all over again. Once devotion was over, I made my way to the pulpit to join the other elders, but I still didn't see Alyssa.

The choir sounded lovely as usual. They all looked exceptional in their new robes. I noticed that there were plenty of new faces this Sunday, but they weren't the detectives. My heart was so warm. When the choir finished their two selections, it was time for me to do the Lord's work. When I came to the pulpit, I saw Alyssa coming down and everything seemed right with the world. Then I hear a loud bang and thought the PA system must be sounding off.

The next thing I remember is waking up in the hospital

surrounded by detectives from the Atlanta Police Department, my mom, and my brother. I think the pain must've jolted me awake. I asked for Alyssa and the baby. I couldn't understand why she would not be y my side. My mom grabbed my hand and asked me if I knew why I was in the hospital, but I have no idea. She explained to me that on Sunday Alyssa had shot Marjorie and turned the gun on me. She told me that the baby is with my sister-in-law. I told mom that had to be some mistake, Alyssa didn't own a gun. It took the detectives to tell me two more times and show me Alyssa's mugshot before I could grasp it. I didn't understand why. Then I started to feel like I failed her as a husband. The cops will just have to come back. I needed some time to process what happened. I asked mom and Daryl to pray with me. Later that night mom informed me that Marjorie did not make it. I just cried. My sweet, beautiful, loving wife had taken a life.

'Death is a tragedy if you've never lived.'

—*Selena Hampton-Peeks*

CPSIA information can be obtained
at www.ICGtesting.com
Printed in the USA
BVHW081351111022
649158BV00004B/580